Everglades Invasion!

Defining the Problem

Seth Matthas

COMPUTER SCIENCE For the REAL World™

Rosen Classroom™

Published in 2018 by The Rosen Publishing Group, Inc.
29 East 21st Street, New York, NY 10010

Book Design: Jennifer Ryder-Talbot
Editor: Caitie McAneney

Photo Credits: Cover Beth Gao/Shutterstock.com; p. 4-5 pisaphotography/Shutterstock.com; p. 5 (mangroves inset) Jesse Kunerth/Shutterstock.com; p. 6 OFFFSTOCK/Shutterstock.com; p. 8 Rich Carey/Shutterstock.com; p. 10 ITTIGallery/Shutterstock.com; p. 11 Saksri Kongkla/Shutterstock.com; p. 12 (alligator inset) 8155069152/Shutterstock.com; p. 12-13 Heiko Kiera/Shutterstock.com; p. 15 Steve Meese/Shutterstock.com; p. 17 Samuel Acosta/Shutterstock.com; p. 18 mariakraynova/Shutterstock.com; p. 20-21 Nick Fox/Shutterstock.com.

Library of Congress Cataloging-in-Publication Data

Names: Matthas, Seth.
Title: Everglades invasion!: defining the problem / Seth Matthas.
Description: New York : Rosen Classroom, 2018. | Series: Computer Kids: Powered by Computational Thinking | Includes glossary and index.
Identifiers: LCCN ISBN 9781508137627 (pbk.) | ISBN 9781538323939 (library bound) | ISBN 9781538355497 (6 pack) | ISBN 9781508137351 (ebook)
Subjects: LCSH: Everglades (Fla.)--Juvenile literature. | Swamp ecology--Florida--Everglades--Juvenile literature. | Swamp animals--Ecology--Florida--Everglades--Juvenile literature.
Classification: LCC F317.E9 M38 2018 | DDC 975.9'39--dc23

Manufactured in the United States of America

CPSIA Compliance Information: Batch #WS18RC: For Further Information contact Rosen Publishing, New York, New York at 1-800-237-9932

Table of Contents

Everglades Ecosystem

The world is full of communities of plants and animals living together. These communities are called ecosystems. Ecosystems include rain forests, deserts, mountains, lakes, oceans, and more. Animals and plants that live together in an ecosystem depend on each other. If a living thing goes **extinct** or is **introduced** into an ecosystem, it has a big effect on other living things.

One important ecosystem in the United States is the Florida Everglades. The Everglades is a wetland ecosystem. It stretches from around Orlando, Florida, south to Florida Bay. There are marshes, swamps, mangroves, and wet prairie in this ecosystem. It's home to the Florida panther, alligators, herons, and manatees. Each part of the ecosystem is important to its survival.

Mangroves are a **species** of tree that provides protection for animals in the Everglades. They also protect the shoreline from **erosion**.

mangroves

Ecosystem in Balance

To keep members of an ecosystem safe, that ecosystem must be healthy. For an ecosystem to be healthy, it must be in balance. What does an ecosystem in balance look like?

Balanced ecosystems have the right amount of plants, prey, and predators. Plants rely on good soil and clean water to grow. Plants provide protection, shelter, and food for animals. They also protect soil from erosion. Predators rely on a certain amount of prey to keep themselves well fed. For example, alligators eat fish, turtles, birds, small mammals, and even other reptiles. A good ecosystem has healthy plants, enough prey for predators, and just enough predators to keep prey populations under control.

There are both alligators and crocodiles in the Everglades. Crocodiles prefer water that is salty, while alligators usually live in freshwater.

Red lionfish came from the South Pacific and Indian Oceans. They are toxic to humans and predators to native fish.

Invasive Species

Many factors can throw an ecosystem out of balance, such as polluted water and air, **deforestation**, or a bad storm. However, one of the greatest **threats** to the Everglades ecosystem comes from invasive species.

Invasive species are plants or animals that are not native to an area and cause harm there. The Everglades is especially at risk because of its climate, or long-term weather patterns. Southern Florida is hot and wet for most of the year. That makes it a great home for many invasive species, especially those from tropical homelands. Native plants and animals are suffering because of invasive species, such as the red lionfish and Burmese python. That's a big problem for the Everglades ecosystem!

The Problem with Invasive Plants

We know that the Everglades ecosystem is suffering because of invasive species. In order to try to solve that problem, wildlife **experts** have to look at the effects of the new species on the ecosystem.

Plants may not be the scariest of all invasive species, but they can do a lot of **damage**. The

The hydrilla weed clogs waters in the Everglades.

National Wildlife Foundation (NWF) says that 1.5 million acres (607,028 ha) of the Everglades suffer from invasive plants. Hydrilla is an **aquatic** weed that harms native plants, makes water quality worse, and reduces water movement. Old world climbing ferns are plants that grow up to 125 feet (38.1 m) tall. They can kill any tree underneath them, including native pine trees.

The Problem with Pythons

Imagine you're walking through Everglades National Park, when all of the sudden, you see a huge python snake! Burmese pythons are not native to the Everglades. They've become a top predator there, which spells trouble for native predators.

Burmese pythons have been known to fight alligators in the Everglades!

Burmese pythons are native to Southeast Asia. People started bringing them to Florida as pets and letting them go once they got too big. As one of the world's largest snakes, this python can reach up to 23 feet (7 m) long. They can slither on land, climb trees, and swim in the water. Small mammals and birds don't stand a chance when a python crosses their path. Wildlife experts noticed that native rabbit populations decreased to nearly nothing once the Burmese python was introduced.

The Problem with Pigs

Wild pigs are a big part of the Everglades invasive species problem. They're also called wild boars, feral hogs, and wild hogs. Wild pigs are not native to South Florida. They came from Europe and Asia, spreading as humans moved to the Americas.

Wild pigs breed, or make babies, very quickly. They cause a lot of harm to ecosystems. That's because they root around for food, using their noses and tusks. This uproots tree and plant sprouts so they can't grow into adulthood. For farmers, wild pigs are a huge issue because they dig up farmland and spread illnesses to livestock. They cause over $800 million in damage to the farming **industry** in the United States. Native plants and animals also suffer greatly.

Wild pigs can live in groups of up to 100 members.

How Did It Happen?

The first step to solving a problem is naming the problem. In this case, the problem is invasive species in the Everglades. The next step to solving a problem is to find out what might have caused it.

How were invasive species introduced to the Everglades? For the most part, invasive species move because of people. People brought wild hogs

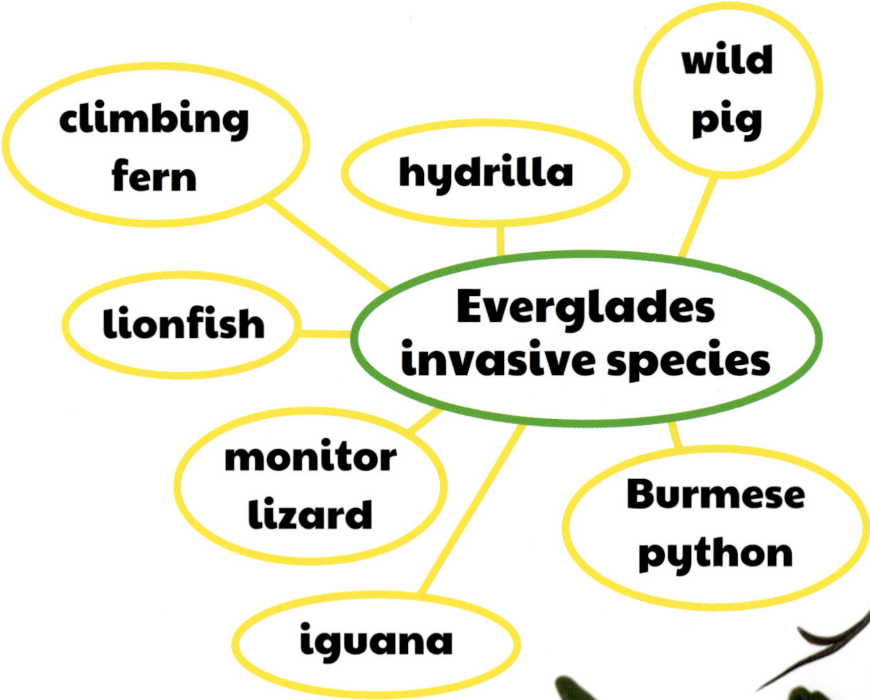

with them when they settled in the Americas. People buy pythons, monitor lizards, and iguanas as pets and then release the large reptiles when they can no longer care for them. Some people grow certain plants in a new location without a thought to the effects it could have on a natural ecosystem.

Florida's position on the coast makes it a point of entry for the reptile and plant trade.

Conservation organizations help to keep natural habitats, like this mangrove forest, safe for the future.

Finding Solutions

Once you know the problem and the cause, you can make a plan to fix the problem. Organizations such as The Nature Conservancy work to protect nature from threats, including invasive species. The Nature Conservancy broke down their plan for helping the Everglades into smaller action steps.

First, they want to prevent invasive species from entering the Everglades in the future. They can do that by working towards laws that keep people from bringing non-native plants and animals to the Everglades. They use tools to predict if a plant species might become invasive. They also can remove animals, such as Burmese pythons, from the Everglades. They help people learn about the dangers of using chemicals on land in the Everglades.

Bringing Back Balance

Is it possible to bring balance back to an ecosystem? We may never know the Everglades as it was before people came there. Once invasive species and pollution take hold in a place, the damage can be hard to reverse. However, there are small steps people can take to make big changes.

Everglades National Park was established in 1947. Making this area a national park was one solution to protecting its natural ecosystem.

One example of people fixing a problem in an ecosystem happened in Yellowstone National Park. In the late 1800s and early 1900s, wolves were hunted to extinction there. The ecosystem was thrown out of balance and suffered. Then, in 1995, wildlife experts released wolves back into the ecosystem. It made the ecosystem become more balanced once again. In the case of the Everglades, removing invasive species might be the answer.

What Can You Do?

The problem of invasive species in the Everglades is a big one. It's being solved by wildlife and **conservation** experts. However, there are things that you can do to be a part of the solution.

You can speak out against the sale of large reptiles, like pythons, as pets. These huge snakes need a lot of care, and they are a risk to people and animals if they are released. You can tell people about invasive species, including invasive plants, to raise awareness. You can visit Everglades National Park to see firsthand what the ecosystem looks like. You can give money to organizations that help keep ecosystems and national parks safe and wild. Knowing about your problem is the first step in solving it!

Glossary

aquatic: Living, growing, or spending time in water.

conservation: The care of the natural world.

damage: Harm.

deforestation: The action or process of clearing forests of trees.

erosion: The act of wearing away by water, wind, or ice.

expert: Someone with great knowledge about a certain subject.

extinct: No longer living.

industry: The businesses that provide a particular product or service.

introduce: To bring something into an area for the first time.

species: A group of plants or animals that are all of the same kind.

threat: Something likely to cause harm.

Index